THE DON'T SWEAT
AFFIRMATIONS

THE DON'T SWEAT
AFFIRMATIONS

100 Inspirations to Help Make Your Life Happier and More Relaxed

By the Editors of Don't Sweat Press
Foreword by Richard Carlson, Ph.D.,
author of the bestselling *Don't Sweat the Small Stuff*

HYPERION

New York

ISBN 0-7868-8712-5

FIRST EDITION

10 9 8 7 6 5 4 3 2 1

Contents

Foreword

Often, the difference between having a good day or a bad one has a lot to do with the types of thoughts that fill our heads and dominate our thinking. Simply put, when our thinking is positive, uplifting, and life-affirming, we feel happy, peaceful and hopeful. On the other hand, when our thoughts are negative, self-defeating, fearful or angry, we tend to feel victimized, overwhelmed and unhappy.

The editors of Don't Sweat Press have put together a book full of inspiring messages to read to yourself. They are simple, but powerful reminders that we have the capacity to live extraordinary lives. By reading these short messages, we are giving ourselves the suggestion to be proactive and grateful. Affirmations such as these remind us of the power that our own thoughts have in shaping our reality and the quality of our lives. When we understand this power, we are more careful about which thoughts we give significance to and which ones we choose to dismiss or ignore.

There is no question that life can be challenging. However, when we take the time to think positive thoughts, and to remember that we, ourselves, are the thinker of those thoughts, we give ourselves the edge we need to stay on track and remain vitalized. It's that little bit of added wisdom that reminds us of what's most important and keeps us from sweating the small stuff.

The affirmations in this book can be a wonderful way to start your day. Or, they can be a welcome break in the midst of chaos. However you choose to best use them, I think you'll agree—they are stress-reducing and a lot of fun. I hope you'll enjoy this book as much as I have, and that you refer to the affirmations often.

Treasure the gift of life,
Richard Carlson
Pleasant Hill, CA, June 2001

THE DON'T SWEAT
AFFIRMATIONS

1.

In the Flow

By choosing to be flexible with problems rather than irritated by them, I allow creative solutions to flow through me.

My mind is at peace, and no problem is too big for me to handle.

I approach every problem with kindness and gentleness.

I do not need to be perfect; only human.

Life is okay the way it is right now.

I treat strangers with kindness and respect.

I take time to be alone, reflect, and enjoy the quiet.

I know that I am loved, and every time I say "I love you," I keep the circle of love alive in the world.

I am calmly centered in the moment and set a good example to those around me.

The uplifting reminders of love that I place around my home remind me that all is well.

I perform every task calmly and peacefully.

I am aware of my changing moods and make allowances for them.

I remain in the moment through every conflict in my life.

The first thing I do every morning and the last before I go to sleep at night is clear my thoughts and simply live in the moment.

I am forgiving and accepting of the people I love, which makes it easier to be myself.

When someone asks me how I am, I respond with calmness rather than reporting how busy I am or listing my problems.

When I keep my cool in the face of little problems that pop up from day to day, I protect my body from stress.

My work is not my entire life. Achieving a goal or finishing a job is wonderful, but every moment contains an opportunity to experience the fullness of life.

When I feel that it's all too much to handle, I lighten up and remind myself that I don't have to be perfect.

I am centered and balanced, and I always bring my mind into the here and now.

My life is filled with harmony, equanimity, and enthusiasm.

With my attention in the moment, I do things calmly and give every task the attention it deserves.

When I am feeling overwhelmed, I imagine that a stranger is taking notes on my behavior and telling me how much unconditional love I am bringing to those around me.

I remain relaxed as drama washes over me.

I handle life's conflicts with clarity and a healthy attitude.

I am flexible and accept changes in my plans with grace.

This moment is the only thing that truly exists. There are no dress rehearsals in life.

I handle the inevitable pressures of life with a calm mind and a relaxed body.

I freely compliment others and spread the joy of life.

I let criticism go and focus on the positive in myself and others.

Taking the small annoyances of the day in stride keeps me free of negativity.

When an unexpected snag comes up during the day, I take a deep, refreshing breath rather than tensing up with frustration.

I am confident in myself and do not need to prove myself to others.

Others appreciate me even more when they experience my genuine humility.

I am an easygoing and peaceful person.

I surrender to the truth of this moment and feel great peace of mind.

My quiet inner voice knows what I need to know, what I need to do, and what changes need to be made in my life.

I am open to what is and do not insist that life be a certain way.

I trust that my intuitive heart will give me all the answers I need.

The powerful force within me is always at work, regardless of what I call it—Higher Spirit, Guardian Angel, Collective Intelligence of the Universe, or God.

I am a good listener, both to my inner voice and to those with whom I live and work.

Rather than living up to the illusion of being "normal," I alone define who I really am.

When I let go of a problem, even for a few seconds, I allow my creative energy to flow toward a solution.

Instead of pushing myself to solve a problem, I relax and keep alert for solutions.

Instead of blowing an annoying scenario out of proportion, I relax and think of the bigger picture.

Nature does not rush its work, and I am part of nature.

I put worried thoughts into proper perspective before they have a chance to run wild and grow out of proportion.

I know that life is not a twenty-four-hour emergency. My work gets done more easily and pleasantly when I am relaxed and confident, rather than tied up in knots of nervous energy.

Life is full of challenges, setbacks, hassles, and obstacles, and the only thing I can control is how I choose to let these things affect me.

I stay calm and centered, regardless of the time or season, and never fall into the frenzied "speed trap" of the holidays.

I control my indulgences, from overspending to overeating, because I am in control of my life.

I keep the experience of universal love present in my life every day.

My life is taking the shape of my dreams every minute of the day.

I believe in the ability to make my own life. There is nothing I cannot do.

I shape my future with a light step and an open heart.

Each morning, I renew my commitment to keep an open heart and an open mind.

One of the gifts I give to others is mindful communication: speaking and listening with patience and love.

I honor the innocence and beauty in others and in myself.

My quiet and calm manner of speaking lowers the collective heart rate, eases up stress hormones, and makes communication more meaningful.

As a mindful communicator, I slow down my speech and let others finish their thoughts.

I am a deliberate listener, pausing to reflect before responding.

I radiate peace and tranquility in the way I speak and listen.

I balance my life completely by nourishing my soul, as well as my mind and body.

I connect to my soul by connecting to what is meaningful in my life.

I find time to enjoy what I love doing the most.

I nurture my soul by spending time with people who uplift and inspire me.

My ordinary life is full of richness and beauty because I am connected to my soul and see the divine in all things.

All of the trappings of success cannot compare with the satisfaction I feel being connected to my internal energy, my soul.

I maintain my inner life like I would maintain an automobile, caring for the hidden parts that keep my life running smoothly.

I live each day as if it were my last, keeping a clear focus on what is truly important.

My mind is connected to my heart, and I think positive, enriching thoughts.

I balance my intellect and my heart and receive peace, strength, and wisdom.

My natural patterns of thought are positive, generous, and loving.

I live up to my commitments and live with integrity, creating a powerful flow of energy between myself and everyone with whom I come into contact.

My mind is always clear and relaxed, an open channel for abundance and joy.

My inner knowing is more powerful than belief. Embracing my own wisdom is an unstoppable formula for producing constructive change, success, and happiness.

I do one thing in the moment and give it my full attention, working with relaxed passion.

I work with positive excitement rather than frenzied worry.

When I stop stress within myself, I prevent the "stress virus" from spreading and create a better world.

All of my actions match my good intentions.

When I pause for inner reflection, I become connected to a deeper intelligence.

I possess an unlimited source of inner wisdom and use reflection to bring it to consciousness.

My energy is abundantly positive and creates positive opportunities and solutions in my life.

I give everything I have to my positive thoughts—they are the strongest force in the world.

What goes around comes around, including the positive energy I create with my thoughts.

I spend my mental energy wisely, on positive thoughts and ideas, and receive dividends beyond my dreams.

I take time to be alone and rejuvenate my peaceful spirit.

When I nurture my soul, I have renewed energy and insight and can approach my life with a lighter, calmer heart.

Living a balanced life includes taking time to do nothing at all.

I have the power to break a cycle of negativity by laughing at an annoying event and lightening the atmosphere.

My inner peace allows me to handle stressful situations with ease.

I approach obstacles with a calm, peaceful, receptive attitude rather than a reactive one.

I shed worry and open myself to joy and abundance.

Solutions come quickly to me, because I take the time to get out of the way and rely on my inner knowledge.

I live in harmony with my higher self, moving effortlessly with the flow of the universe.

I do not let the fast pace of life affect my calm and solid foundation of inner peace and strength.

I hope with all my heart that everyone expands to their greatest potential, including myself. There is room enough in the world for everyone to succeed.

I celebrate milestones in other people's lives because every time someone succeeds, it helps the rest of us.

My balance of mind and soul allows me to tap into the unlimited potential of the universe.

Opportunity exists everywhere I look.

2.

Problems as Opportunities

When I keep a broad perspective of the world around me, my everyday problems become ordinary tasks rather than major dramas.

I refuse to compound a problem by focusing on my mistake. I take my error lightly, learn from it, and move on.

I respond to challenges with perspective and grace, because I know that life isn't meant to be hassle-free or perfect.

A larger perspective prevents me from indulging in petty things.

I do not resist life, but instead turn problems into opportunities for growth.

When I make a mistake, I am grateful for the opportunity to learn how to do something better.

I have more energy to solve my problems, because I struggle with them less.

I redefine a problem as a lesson, asking myself why the issue is in my life and what I can learn from it.

I achieve true happiness by changing my relationship with my problems, not by getting rid of them.

Problems are a potential source of awakening.

An obstacle can help me practice patience and open myself to a life of growth and peace.

I set healthy boundaries and limits—I don't automatically take other people's problems upon myself.

I spend more time accepting problems as a natural part of my life than running away from them.

Life is more like a dance than a battle when I accept obstacles as opportunities.

I approach even the most painful issues with my partner in a heart-to-heart manner, opening the way for mutual understanding and deeper intimacy.

I do not confuse personal feelings of frustration with problems in my relationships. Rather than looking outward, I turn within and find the source of my discomfort.

Instead of simply reacting in frustration or anger, I view my problems in a softer way, with a genuine desire to learn from them.

Transforming my problems into unique sources for growth lifts a great weight from my shoulders.

I blame no one but myself for my problems.

I hold all the keys to solving my problems.

All obstacles are potential teachers.

I focus on the positive steps I am taking to overcome my problems rather than on the negative aspects of the problems themselves.

My focus on the positive in all situations makes life more interesting.

I practice calm surrender rather than struggling against things that are beyond my control.

Calm surrender eases the chaos and invites solutions.

My practice of staying in the here and now keeps my mind clear to find a solution to any problem.

There is a positive pathway through every obstacle. My higher self is ready and willing to give me all the answers that I need.

With deeper peace of mind, my melodramas have been transformed into "mellow-dramas."

I stay relaxed in the face of conflict and handle everything with grace and clarity.

When my mind moves too quickly, I have the power to stop, relax, breathe deeply, and reconnect with my soul.

I put life's problems on the back burner of my mind, where my higher intelligence can go to work on them.

Solutions come effortlessly and naturally to me.

Time moves at a more leisurely pace when I approach my problems and my work in a relaxed, peaceful state of mind.

I have the power to thoroughly transform my problem-solving methods.

Every challenge and obstacle is a custom-made opportunity to help me learn something about life and about myself.

My problems are gifts rather than hindrances.

I trust my intuitive heart to lead me in the direction of solutions, happiness, and well-being.

I surrender to life as it is, not as it should be.

Each challenge, like each moment, contains clarity and truth that can revitalize my life.

Calm surrender opens me to wisdom.

I have perfect trust in the quiet voice within me.

I see humor in my fruitless efforts and cheerfully leave them behind.

My problems help me burn away the rough parts of myself and become all that I can be.

I am totally honest with myself and accept that I have created my own circumstances.

The knowledge that I have the power to create my circumstances proves that I have the power to change them.

I forgive myself for my mistakes, and I am grateful for what they have taught me.

When I feel overwhelmed by problems, I remember that new seeds begin growing in darkness before springing to life. Even in the most difficult times, good things are ripening beneath the surface.

My mind is connected to my heart, and it is effortless to think positive, productive thoughts that lead to solutions.

I trust the universe and my own inner resources to help me with every challenge.

When I admit that I don't know what to do, I allow my inner wisdom and guidance to take over.

I accept the fact that problems will always come into my life and things are going to go wrong. This realization helps me react with wisdom and insight rather than worry and panic.

By sharing positive thoughts and feelings with my friends and loved ones, I break the chain of complaining and whining that can bring down the energy in a room or a household.

I am responsive rather than reactive, always ready to find creative solutions.

I transcend my problems by calling upon my higher self to solve them.

Using my inner wisdom, I can see solutions that my reactive, emotional self cannot.

My role at work and in my home is to be a stress stopper, not a stress spreader.

I am open, willing, and excited about finding creative solutions to my problems.

My problems do not define me; how I react to them tells people who I am.

I am connected to a deeper intelligence that speaks to me when I go within myself with humility.

My mind is a creative space filled with solutions, possibilities, and inspirations.

My positive energy draws positive circumstances and people into my life.

I set the stage for creative solutions and exciting new opportunities with a positive outlook and a light heart.

I possess the ability to change anything in my life.

I do not fear asking for help when my intuitive heart leads me to someone who has the wisdom to give me the advice and assistance I need.

I keep my perspective and sense of humor in the face of adversity.

I am open and lighthearted, even when confronted with obstacles, and I always learn from my mistakes.

I recognize the critical shifts in life and move with them rather than keeping blindly to one path.

With an open mind and intuitive heart, I tap into the deeper wisdom we all share.

Some problems are signals that it's time to leave the old and start off in a new direction. Without this challenge, I could be caught on a nonproductive track for weeks, months, or years.

I do not place blame outwardly, but accept responsibility for the results in my life. Every time I overcome an obstacle or meet a challenge, I reaffirm that I have access to all solutions and develop a deeper trust in my inner resources.

In times of conflict, I am forgiving and patient with myself.

Conflicts and obstacles are essential to self-growth.

Like many scientists and creative people, I am ready to let go and hear the solution to my problem in a dream, daydream, or flashing thought.

I open my eyes in the morning with love in my heart, ready to greet every event of the day with patience, open-mindedness, and gratitude.

I respect the universe for creating challenges that will help me grow and become the most powerful and loving person I can be.

I do not play the blame game; instead, I embrace every experience in my life as a path to growth and development.

My problems are really opportunities for learning how to open my heart.

I trust the universe to place a silver lining in every challenge of my life.

No matter what comes up in my life, I know that "this, too, will pass."

Problems are not only inevitable but an important part of life.

I am flexible and open to looking at my problems from a new perspective.

I no longer react to problems with fear, but face them with a sense of adventure.

I measure my success by how well I face my problems, not by how long I can avoid them.

No matter how overwhelming my problems appear, there is a solution for every one of them.

I am in charge of every challenge—and triumph—in my life.

With every problem I work through, I become wiser.

Staying calm in the face of adversity is one of the greatest accomplishments of my life.

When the same problem comes up again and again, I remind myself that it is my thinking that is flawed, not my life.

Every problem contains an opportunity for personal growth.

I am a strong, independent person whose challenges spur me on to grow and thrive.

Dealing with my problems keeps me productive in all areas of my life.

The universe sends me joy, as well as problems, to make my life journey worthwhile.

Conflicts and challenges bring out the best in me.

I face my problems with grace and dignity and provide a positive example for others.

As I work through a problem, I move closer to my full potential.

The challenges in my life help me understand others more deeply.

I take responsibility for my problems, but do not dwell on them or complain about them to others.

Focusing on the positive at all times helps me find solutions to problems.

When I stop doing and sit still, I allow answers to pop into my mind.

Life is exactly as it should be, with all its problems and its joys.

3.

Quiet Mind

Letting go of a problem allows my creative energy to flow toward a solution.

I take time to rejuvenate myself in silence.

Being alone for a few moments every day helps balance the noise and stimuli of the day.

My life is vastly improved and enhanced when I rise early and surround myself with peace and quiet.

Taking time to relax my mind and body is as important to success as working on my goals.

When my head is free of concerns and annoyances, I can do every task with more energy and efficiency.

My quiet mind is the foundation of inner peace.

Inner peace translates into outer peace, affecting every aspect of my life.

I become what I practice. Repeated practice of sitting in silence and quieting my thoughts leads to deep peace.

I bring forth the quality of calm and well-being by nurturing my inner peace.

I clear my mind of negative thoughts and allow positive, peaceful thoughts to enter.

My mind is capable of much more than thinking, worrying, and remembering.

Nurturing my inner peace affects not only my life, but the lives of those near me.

I do not have to be doing something every moment of the day.

Every moment I spend in quiet contemplation brings healthy balance to my busy, over-stimulated life.

I do not need to focus on something or be entertained every moment.

I do not anticipate boredom when I sit in silence. I do not anticipate anything.

I have the patience to let go of my thoughts for a few moments and practice having a quiet mind.

My overactive mind longs for silence.

Practicing quiet and meditation helps me handle the inevitable pressures of life with a more relaxed mind.

When my mind moves too quickly, I take a moment to sit quietly, breathe deeply, and focus on the present.

A quiet mind pours into everything I do.

Taking time to be quiet and think of nothing is one of the best gifts I give myself.

Devoting time to practicing quiet does not make me any less responsible for my work or family, but helps me approach them with more energy and peace.

My foundation of inner peace helps me sort out the small stuff from the other stuff.

My quiet voice speaks the loudest.

Meditation helps me develop lightness of being and a harmonious life.

My day runs more smoothly when I take a moment to close my eyes in quiet contemplation.

Developing a practice of quiet mind feeds my soul.

My inner life deserves to be nourished by sitting in silence.

My quiet mind is as important to my life as my thinking mind.

I cannot think my way to happiness. Nourishment for the soul comes from the heart, and when I release my thoughts in quiet contemplation, I open myself to knowing from my heart.

Developing quiet inner confidence gives me the strength and wisdom to let go and refrain from trying to control the events and people around me.

Practicing having a quiet mind helps me get in touch with my rich inner resources.

I connect with my inner wisdom by taking the time to quiet my mind.

My moments of quiet reflection help me get out of the way and allow answers to arise from within.

My quiet mind is a peaceful oasis that I can visit at any time.

My life energy is charged like a battery every time I sit in silence.

I practice quiet contemplation for my mind and regular exercise for my body.

My hardworking brain deserves a break in the form of silent contemplation.

I am fortified by my practice of quiet mind and do not get upset by little things.

I define the pace of my life.

Developing the patience and discipline to quiet my mind is a great accomplishment.

I sit in silence as a gesture of respect to my soul.

My inner wisdom bubbles up in periods of quiet contemplation.

My capacity to love deepens when I tap into the silence of my inner self.

The silence of meditation helps me reconnect with my soul.

Meditation is my inner adventure.

My contemplative mind delivers as much important information as my thinking mind.

My soul deserves my devoting a few minutes every day to silence.

I value my quiet moments as much as I value being with those I love.

My inner vision is clear and available.

I am at peace with the universe.

My inner being always leads me on the right path.

My quiet mind is receptive to the limitless ideas flowing through
the universe.

I love my quiet mind and nourish it in silence.

All aspects of my being, both visible and invisible, are vibrant and
alive.

My foundation of inner peace allows me to accept whatever life has to offer.

Every moment I spend in quiet stillness brings me closer to my true self.

My practice of quiet mind enriches my life in ways that no material object or money can enrich it.

When I practice sitting in silence, I join a timeless tradition of wisdom.

I am filled with silence and peace.

Quite contemplation brings harmony to my work and my home.

Calming my mind is an act of love.

When I don't indulge in small annoyances, I have more energy to do productive things.

When I keep small problems small, I have more time to experience the magic and beauty of life.

When I feel bogged down by a problem, I take a few seconds to remember the miracle of just being alive.

Every moment of silence is a leap into the unknown.

I can return to the quiet mindfulness of my childhood—when I was absorbed in drawing or reading, for instance—at any time.

Even in my sleep, my mind is busy with dreams. Consciously practicing a quiet mind is a gift I give to my overworked self.

A still mind is the source of all my goodness.

When I contact the well of peace that lies within, I lose all fear.

Each time I pause to go within, I draw closer to who I really am.

I cleanse my mind of thoughts and bathe it in silence.

The greatest fulfillment of my life comes from going within and connecting with my soul.

Practicing silence helps me draw strength from my source and drive away mental and physical weakness.

I approach the silent voice inside with reverence and respect.

Every time I sit in silence, I become more accustomed to relying on my inner resources.

I am not a slave to my thoughts or emotions.

I can easily contact my inner silence, even in the midst of work or other activities.

My mind is light and joyful.

I have the ability to discern what is best for me because I listen to the quiet voice within, which always knows what is right and what is good.

Sitting in silence helps clear my mind, which is a conduit for all knowledge.

I fill my head with positive thoughts and high ideals, and this results in great success in every area of my life.

I am empowered by the energy I draw from my inner self.

Being in touch with my soul helps me develop affection, sincerity, generosity, and cheerfulness.

I sit in silence to open the doors of wisdom and light that exist inside me.

I am grateful for every moment that I spend in silence, and vow to keep this practice.

I continue to take the time to sit in quiet reflection almost every day, and do not get discouraged if I backslide and skip the practice now and then. The longing I have to be quiet and still is a sign from my inner self that I am on the right path.

I am always relaxed, calm, and ready to listen to my inner voice.

I do not require anyone or anything to give me peace of mind. Perfect calm exists within me.

I respect and acknowledge the calm, inner well of wisdom that resides in everyone I see.

Each moment I spend in silence is a gift I give to myself and others.

The last thing I do before going to sleep is give thanks for the constant wisdom and support that flowed from within me throughout the day.

I put complete trust in my higher self and eagerly look forward to connecting with it every day.

I am blessed with a consciousness that can focus on my inner life.

My ideal moment is sitting in silence, listening to my inner voice and deriving strength from the unlimited resources of the universe.

There is no conflict that I cannot resolve by listening to my inner voice.

The essence of my soul is simplicity, silence, and love.

The serenity of my inner being flows into everything I do and lies beneath every word I speak.

4.

Power to Choose

This moment, I decide to be happy.

There will always be problems and challenges to meet, but I no longer use them to postpone my happiness.

I am not molded in steel, but instead am flexible and open to change.

When I face an annoying situation, I choose to be kind.

My future is unfolding according to the dreams and goals I choose right now.

I replace my old patterns of reaction with new habits of perspective.

I have the power to choose how I respond to everything that comes into my life.

My habits are not permanent.

I see something good in everyone.

I live my life as a gift, not as a to-do list.

I choose to bring forth kindness, love, and compassion in my life.

When confronted with gossip or talking behind someone's back, I choose to keep silent.

My mind attracts positive thoughts and words like a magnet.

I appreciate the life in this moment, just as it is.

I voice my love and support for others rather than assuming that they know how I feel.

I try to treat others—all others—as I would like them to treat me.

I choose to approach my work calmly and allow my inner peace to flow out around me.

When faced with a choice, I try to do the most loving thing.

When I choose to be generous, I ultimately receive more.

I choose to be human rather than perfect.

I love myself unconditionally.

I choose to be supportive rather than critical.

I am aware of my anger, and choose to transform it into forgiveness and understanding.

I let go of resentments and other small stuff from the past.

I accept change as a positive force in life.

I take care of myself as I would take care of a beloved child.

I choose to be calm rather than frantic when my day gets hectic.

I focus on the positive things I've learned after making mistakes.

My future is filled with the abundance and joy I choose for myself today.

I alleviate stress in my body and my environment rather than adding to it.

From this moment, I choose to let go of one bad habit and free my life energy for higher things.

Whenever I catch myself dwelling on the past, I choose to let it go and focus on the present and the infinite possibilities of the future.

When people criticize me, I choose to see a lesson in their words and be grateful for the opportunity to grow from them.

I try to be humble and sincere, and have no need to boast or complain.

I choose to soften my most critical positions and transform them with a larger perspective.

I choose to distance myself from those who dwell on the negative and pollute the atmosphere with cynicism.

In every conversation, I choose to listen rather than running through my own inner dialogue.

My life is a reflection of my choices.

When I choose selfishness, my world becomes small and stifled; when I choose generosity, my world expands beyond all boundaries.

I choose the path that reveals itself to me through my intuition.

When I am surrounded by negativity or am in a stressful situation, I choose to keep a light heart and tap into my inner peace.

I let go of old, habitual, self-defeating thoughts.

I surround myself with people who love and appreciate life.

I choose to be loving and accepting of people.

I know that I am more than this body, and I invite my higher self to work in my life. In a stressful situation, I call upon this greater self to do the right thing.

I choose patience over intolerance, kindness over a self-serving attitude.

I am the architect of my life, and I choose joy, prosperity, love, and soulfulness.

I choose to learn from the wisdom of my dreams.

I choose to find something beautiful in every scene I pass today.

Before I go to sleep, I choose to let go of all of my problems and concerns for the night and hand them over to the universe.

I make decisions that resonate from my heart.

I choose to mold my life to my inner wisdom rather than to society's expectations.

I create my own definition of success and spend every day joyfully working toward my goals.

When I feel overwhelmed, I stop and find the humor in my situation. I choose to laugh at the outrageous things I get myself into.

I choose to set my own peaceful pace during the holidays.

I take a few moments every day to remind myself that I am loved, protected, and free.

I focus on the unstoppable, miraculous life energy in my body.

I choose to let love and light enter my heart, and to remember that I am never alone.

When I find myself procrastinating, I ask my higher self to give me the discipline to move on and delve into the joy of work.

I choose to accept whatever comes my way at this moment with a peaceful spirit.

I live up to my responsibilities and live every day with honor.

I choose to be less reactive and deal with situations with patience and integrity.

I am open to every opportunity the universe puts in my path.

I choose to be at peace so that I can hear opportunity knocking.

I choose to see the big picture and keep myself from getting wrapped up in my small problems.

I choose to listen to my inner wisdom rather than blindly following things that other people have told me.

I approach everything I do with love.

When I am truly absorbed in what I'm doing, I am productive, creative, and fully alive.

I choose to release worry from my mind.

I approach my work with relaxed passion, finding excitement rather than stress in the challenges that present themselves.

I let go of worry and free myself to see stressful situations in a new light.

I choose openness and curiosity over cynicism.

I choose to refrain from making important decisions when I am stressed or feeling low.

I have the power to choose what is important and what is small stuff in my life.

I choose to spend my mental energy on the positive and watch it create abundance and happiness in my life and in the lives of those around me.

I embrace wealth consciousness and release all financial worries.

I use my mind for positive change—a workable solution, a better alternative, or a productive plan—rather than wasting my mental energy criticizing and pointing out faults.

I know what I want, and I have the self-determination and confidence to ask for it.

I release my fear of rejection.

I have every right to ask for help.

I am able to do more for others when I am doing the best that I possibly can.

I choose to align myself with the strongest force—positive energy.

My positive attitude is building an exciting, abundant, and harmonious future. The positive thoughts I have now will reap undreamed-of rewards in the future.

I choose to think big and open myself to all possibilities.

I choose to slow the chatter in my mind and listen to the directions that the winds of change bring into my life.

I make choices from my own inner knowing and live my own life.

I choose to pause and reflect, rather than reacting to problems with anger and aggressiveness.

I choose to deal with the day-to-day tasks of my home life with calm surrender, knowing that there will always be more to do, and focusing on one thing at a time.

I choose to open myself to a steady flow of positive energy.

The core of my life is freedom of choice, and my life is not determined by the past, but instead is shaped by the thoughts I have right now.

I choose to be perfectly at ease and trust that everything is as it should be.

I am confident that all is well in the universe, and I have no fear or uncertainty.

I choose to allow my splendid uniqueness to shine in the world.

I choose to always bring my wandering mind back to positive, loving thoughts.

Everything is working together toward the perfect good today and always.

I choose to see my life as a miracle, relishing my friendships, loved ones, opportunities for work and growth, and all the natural beauty that surrounds me.

I choose to be an example of sincerity, honesty, integrity, and positive energy.

I choose to take control of situations in my life with a calm, peaceful attitude.

I am forgiving and patient with myself.

I make my life simpler by choice rather than by need, practicing voluntary simplicity.

I define my results and allow my inner wisdom to tell me when it's time to persevere and when it's time to do something differently.

5.

Gratitude

I am grateful for what I have and for being alive.

I am grateful for my work and find joy in doing even the smallest task of the day.

I am aware of the perfection of life itself.

I spend a moment each day thinking of someone to thank.

Waking up with gratitude on my mind each morning, I begin the day with a feeling of peace.

I have a loving heart that is grateful for the smallest things, from having a door opened for me to a stranger giving me a smile.

Feeling gratitude puts me in a state of calm and openness.

I pause many times every day to be thankful for my work and for all the love in my life.

I choose to appreciate everything life brings me, and as my gratitude deepens, I feel more in harmony with my surroundings and with the people in my life.

At the close of each day, I take a moment to reflect and be grateful.

I feel blessed to be alive.

I am grateful to be God's guest on this beautiful planet.

I feel grateful when I feel well, and try to act gracefully when I am not feeling well.

This moment, I close my eyes, take a deep breath, and remember all I have to be grateful for.

I focus on being thankful for what I have, rather than complaining about what I do not have.

I see the extraordinary in the ordinary.

I am in awe of the miraculous life that flows through my body and keeps it alive.

Every type of life is precious, and I am grateful to be surrounded by people, plants, animals, and all living things.

Counting my blessings helps me focus my mind on what is right in my life.

When my heart is filled with gratitude, I cannot help but have a wonderful day.

I am fortunate to live on this earth and to have the opportunity to love and be loved.

I am grateful for my ability to feel and express emotions—to laugh with my family and friends, to feel love, to be moved by music and art, and to spread the joy in my heart.

I stop at this moment to remind myself that I'm glad to be alive.

I am fortunate to be able to create the life I want.

I begin every day contemplating something for which I am grateful.

A sense of gratitude nourishes my soul.

When someone does something for me or makes me happy, I express my gratitude and spread my happiness. Sincere gratitude is contagious.

I do not wait for bad news to make me appreciate my life, and I do not take the small miracles for granted. I am deeply grateful for laughter, friendship, beauty, fresh air, and the sun shining through the trees.

Looking at the world with eyes of gratitude gives me a larger and more loving perspective.

Life is fragile, and I am grateful for each precious moment.

A sense of gratitude fills my heart with heightened awareness.

The more I express my gratitude, the more I realize what I have to be grateful for.

Evidence of goodness surrounds me at every turn.

At this moment, my body is performing countless activities to keep me healthy and alive, all without my asking.

My grateful heart is a source of joy to myself and others.

I understand the power of a simple yet sincere "thank you," and I never miss an opportunity to spread this form of positive energy.

There will never be another day like this one.

I am grateful for this new day, in which I have more opportunities to grow and become more loving.

I appreciate the emotional support that I receive from my family and friends, and I tell them so.

I take this moment to thank God for giving me life.

I am grateful for my inner wisdom, which is always pouring out solutions and advice.

I accept the fresh ideas that are flowing toward me, and I am grateful for having an open mind with which to receive them.

Every second of my life is a gift.

I am grateful for the energy that feeds my creativity.

I am grateful for the opportunity to work toward my full potential.

I feel my breath go in and out, and I am grateful for the process.

Every morning, I am grateful for a new day to learn and to earn a living.

I appreciate the help and support of everyone who helped me get where I am today.

I am grateful for the rights and freedoms I enjoy as part of this society.

When I go to a movie, watch television, or listen to the radio, I am grateful for the wonderful forms of entertainment that are available to me at all times.

I appreciate the small acts of kindness that greet me every day, at work, at the store, in school, at home, on the road, and on the street.

I am grateful for the telephone and other technologies that allow me to be in touch with those that I love.

I am thankful for all of my teachers.

When I see the sunshine during the day and the stars at night, my heart is filled with gratitude for this amazing universe.

A sincere "thank you" lets people know that I respect and appreciate them.

I always have enough time to thank people for their help and kindness, no matter how small their act was.

I do not take my home, my job, or my transportation for granted.

Before eating, I take a few seconds to pause and thank the universe for sustaining me.

I am thankful for the love and companionship of my pets.

I am grateful for the environment that gives me oxygen to breathe, the ground to walk upon, and the wilderness to enjoy.

I am grateful for my body's ability to heal.

I am grateful for all the farmers who grow food for the world.

Feeling gratitude puts me in a state of reflection that nourishes my soul.

When my heart is filled with gratitude, I am more open to the joy of life.

I am grateful for the ability to keep the small stuff small and refrain from worrying about every challenge that comes into my day.

Every time I hear the cry of a baby or the voice of a child, I feel grateful for the continuity of life.

I am grateful for my ability to read and for all the books that have brought me inspiration, wisdom, and understanding.

At this moment, I pause to be thankful for what I am doing and where I am right now.

My sense of gratitude is a sign of the love that I have for all things.

I release old resentments, and I am thankful for every experience I have had.

I thank the Creator for giving me the ability to reflect, learn, grow, and develop to my greatest potential.

I am grateful for all of my senses: the ability to smell flowers and fresh cotton sheets; to see the faces of those that I love and the glories of nature; to feel the world with my fingertips; to hear music and voices; and to taste the foods of the earth.

I am thankful for having an open heart that can feel love and compassion.

As I go about my day, I stop to focus on my breath and feel gratitude for all of the unseen miracles going on in my body.

I am grateful for the sound of birds singing in the morning.

I am grateful for the wisdom to let go of problems rather than resisting them.

I remind myself of the big picture throughout the day, and I am grateful for the opportunity to be alive every moment.

I am grateful for the ability to turn inward and find peace rather than allowing the small annoyances of life to get me down.

I am grateful for my inner longing to connect with my soul.

Every spark of insight that inspires me makes me a more compassionate and loving person and affects everyone around me.

I am grateful for the ability to listen to my heart, not just my head.

I release old habits of pessimism and cynicism, and choose to be grateful.

My heightened awareness makes me discover more to be grateful for.

Every step forward in my life deepens my gratitude for all things.

I am thankful for the opportunity to make a difference in my life today, whether it is by simply sharing love through a smile, facing a controversy with kindness, physically helping someone, or holding others in my positive thoughts.

I am grateful to the universe for helping me to solve problems, thereby burning away my old habits.

I am grateful for the love I am receiving at this moment.

I am thankful for the people who come into my life to share different points of view and enlarge my perspective.

I have the ability to make wise, productive decisions, and I am grateful for being able to listen to my inner knowledge.

I am grateful for the ability to send love at this moment.

I have the discipline to move forward toward my dreams with confidence and joy.

I value my silent time, and I am grateful for my inner oasis of peace and serenity.

I am thankful for everyone who has provided a positive example in my life. I will take a moment right now to remember one person who has inspired me.

There is nothing ordinary in this world, and I am grateful for my unique personality and gifts.

I release my attitude of being a victim, and I am grateful for the knowledge that all power to change resides in me.

I am grateful for my limitless inner resources.

I am thankful for the expanding journey that unfolds before me every moment.

I hold the highest vision for myself and for everyone. There is plenty of room in this universe for all to reach their greatest happiness and highest potential.

My priorities are clear, and I am grateful for the ability to pour all my energy into the important things in life: sharing love and becoming aware of my connection to all people and all things.

6.

Abundance

Every aspect of my life is an extension of my consciousness.
My wealth consciousness is my blueprint for prosperity.

I have everything I need right now.

I release all feelings of jealousy and envy toward others, opening
my heart to all good things.

My success does not depend on the failure of someone else.
I sincerely wish great success and happiness for everyone.

Opportunities knock more than once, and I release feelings of frustration about past opportunities.

I release my old belief that there is not enough to go around.

With every layer of fear and anxiety that I lose, I gain more energy and creativity.

My positive thoughts are capable of creating anything.

The only limit to my financial success resides in my limited thoughts.

Letting go of old beliefs about money is an exciting challenge, and I am ready to change my life forever.

Money is only one of the currencies of life.

I deserve to have the financial resources to care for myself and those that I love.

Being prosperous gives me the ability to support causes that I care about.

When I develop wealth consciousness, my prosperity spreads out into the world and helps others.

Financial prosperity is a result of my wealth consciousness, not the other way around.

I trust in the universe and my own inner resources.

My prosperity is not dependent upon my job or my career, but upon my deep belief that the unlimited resources of the universe are mine.

By being prosperity-conscious, true abundance is just around the corner.

When I focus my mind on prosperity, it expands in my outer life.

I release worry about financial problems and make room for my prosperity antennae to catch all opportunities for abundance.

My mind is open to receive all the gifts of the universe.

I release the thought that there is anything lacking in the universe or in my life.

I am thankful for all the services available to me, and I write my checks with a sense of gratitude. I am blessed to have electricity, water, food, a home, clothing, and transportation.

I am thankful for all the services that my tax payments support, and am grateful to live in this free society.

I am proud to support my democratic form of government.

My mind embraces financial prosperity.

I release all thoughts of limitation.

The calm, secure feeling of wealth consciousness fills my mind.

I think about my finances with a joyful heart.

I try to meet all of my financial obligations.

The universe's energy flows through my life.

I cheerfully accept all the responsibilities of managing money.

I feel the joy of watching my abundance enrich the world.

No outer force is blocking my abundance. Obstacles are only figments of my imagination, and I clear them away in an instant with a positive thought.

Every flash of intuition reminds me that my inner resources are all-knowing and all-powerful.

I am capable of creating the abundance I desire with the power of my positive thoughts.

My mind gravitates toward abundance and releases thoughts of limitation.

Everything I do is productive and successful.

I put my heart into everything I do, and I am rewarded well for my work.

I am surrounded and supported by a limitless universe.

Every positive thought returns to me in the many forms that love takes: emotions, positive energy, and material prosperity.

I swing open the doors to wealth consciousness and clear my mind of all doubts.

My soul is connected to the abundance of the universe.

My mind is at peace, and I have complete confidence that my finances are prosperous and growing.

The nature of the universe is expansion, and my wealth consciousness expands every moment.

Nurturing my positive thoughts about money is one of the most virtuous things I can do for myself and for those that I love.

The generosity of the Creator expresses itself through me.

I am a vehicle for the abundance of the universe to flow into the world.

I release the negative attitudes toward money that I learned as a child.

I have the power to transform my thoughts about money.

My positive attitude takes form in the physical world.

Worries about money are small stuff that I now overcome with positive thoughts.

Wealth consciousness is a gift from my inner wisdom. I choose to accept this gift and use it wisely for the good of all.

My old limited beliefs about money are part of the clutter that I now have the opportunity to clear out. My future holds undreamed-of prosperity.

The ceiling of my prosperity is defined by my thoughts. I choose to think big.

Money is a positive force that enriches lives and makes wonderful things happen.

I spend my money wisely and respect all of my obligations.

All of the petty, negative beliefs that used to hamper my prosperity are now burned away in the bright light of my positive thoughts.

I am grateful for the opportunity to draw money into my life with my positive thoughts.

I do everything I can, every day, to bring positive energy into my life and into the lives of those that I love.

I am perfectly capable of supporting the good causes that ask for my support.

My generosity reaches further into the world when I have financial abundance.

The unlimited abundance of the universe desires to flow through me.

Developing wealth consciousness is part of my personal growth and brings me in touch with the limitless nature of my soul.

I am generous and eager to share my abundance with the world.

I do not look to others to fulfill my dreams, but instead have complete trust in my inner resources.

Every building, invention, work of art, or material object began as the same thing: a thought. My financial abundance is being built through my positive thoughts at this very moment.

I trust my inner being to lead me to every opportunity for financial abundance.

I try to be generous with everything I have, from money to creative ideas to loving thoughts.

Every positive thought I have adds to my prosperity consciousness.

I am eager to see the forms that my new wealth consciousness will take in the world around me.

My financial abundance allows me to create a better world.

I deserve to be a vehicle for the positive energy of the universe— it flows through me and through all of the things I do.

My mind is "wired" for wealth consciousness.

I lavishly immerse my mind in thoughts of abundance, prosperity, generosity, and goodness.

Any disharmony in my life is the result of a negative thought. I release my negative thoughts about money, and open my mind to all of the positive resources in the universe.

The Creator supplies me abundantly.

This moment, I change my mind from thoughts of lack to thoughts of prosperity.

Changing my consciousness changes my life.

I attract prosperity into my life with every positive thought and action.

When people succeed, I am as happy for them as I would be for my own success. I congratulate others for putting their prosperity consciousness to work, and I am inspired by their success.

It is my choice to live in abundance.

My life is firmly established in the prosperity of the universe.

Everything I see reminds me of the unlimited energy and goodness of the universe.

The positive energy of the universe is the same power that runs my body and brings all good things into my life.

I take time every day to close my eyes, focus on the abundance of the universe, and open my mind to the awareness of unlimited prosperity.

I am truly grateful for my ever-expanding awareness of love, security, and prosperity.

My natural state is one of peace, harmony, overflowing abundance, and love.

The universe is always giving.

Prosperity is always available; I simply need to be open and receive it.

I release my resistance to the good things of life and open myself to allow energy to flow through me in the form of love, work, creativity, and money.

Abundance is one form of energy, and I use the energy of my positive thoughts to draw money into my life.

The universe richly supplies me when I do what I love.

I express gratitude for everything that I have, which opens me more fully to the abundance that surrounds me.

I choose to focus on the good in my life with gratitude and an open heart, joyfully anticipating all the good to come.

I always hold the highest vision of who I am and why I am here. There are no limits to what I can do.

I am rich in ideas, intelligence, friendship, inspiration, and inner wisdom.

Abundance comes to me easily.

Every positive thought of mine is an expression of my soul. When I focus on any form of goodness, including financial abundance, I am expressing the goodness of the universe.

7.

Kindness

The more kind and gentle I am, the more positive energy I bring to my home, my job, and the world.

I am kind to myself by forgiving myself for mistakes and being grateful for having learned from them.

I greet strangers with kindness and meet their eyes as a natural extension of my loving heart.

My acts of loving-kindness release the emotional equivalent of endorphins, fueling my capacity to love.

I choose to transform criticism and self-defeating thoughts into kindness and positive energy.

Being kind is a powerful expression of love in the world.

The greatest spiritual leaders of the world practice kindness and humility, and my kind acts bring me closer to my ideal self.

My random acts of kindness connect me to my soul and energize my life.

When I practice random acts of kindness, I am living from the heart.

The joy of giving to others is one of the greatest gifts I can give to myself.

When I do something kind, without expecting anything in return, I am truly alive.

I view every meeting with another person—at work, at the store, in class, on the bus—as an opportunity for kindness.

I take time every day to focus on one of the most important ideas in any language: Be kind.

In every situation, I ask myself if there is any way I can express kindness.

I have a conscious choice to react with kindness, and I choose this path every time.

Every time I smile, I spread kindness and positive energy into the world.

I remember that being kind, even in small ways, is a powerful force for clearing away negativity.

Random acts of kindness make the world a better place.

The secrets of love reveal themselves to me when I act with kindness.

I do everything I can to spread the contagious spirit of kindness to my workplace, my home, and every environment in which I find myself.

One of my small acts of kindness may be the positive force that turns someone's life around today.

There is no limit to my kindness, as the source of my kindness is the bottomless well of my soul.

I interact kindly and positively with people, and this brings wonderful friendships and opportunities into my life.

My loving, generous heart stimulates me to do random acts of kindness every day.

I am deeply grateful for the small acts of kindness given to me.

I open myself to generosity of spirit so that my genuine kindness can make a difference in someone's life today.

When I uplift someone's spirit with kindness, I improve the world.

My soul is always ready to react to a situation with kindness, and I open my heart to listen to this inner wisdom.

I choose to show that I care, rather than just saying that I care.

Kindness is a central part of my spiritual practice.

I clear my mind of resentment, grudges, and other negative thoughts so that my natural state of generosity and kindness can shine through.

My acts of kindness spring from my loving attitude toward the world.

A simple act of kindness is the easiest gift to give, and I freely spread kindness to everyone I meet.

Witnessing kindness in action touches my heart.

Helping others increases my feelings of self-worth and value in this world. I am always needed, because there is always someone who needs an act of kindness.

The effects of my simple acts of kindness ripple into the world and reach much further than I can imagine.

I choose to be respectful and considerate.

I release my childish acts of selfishness and impatience and replace them with attitudes of kindness, humility, and warmth.

Kind acts create a gracious living environment. My genuine kindness produces positive energy in the world around me.

Being nice to people is not a weakness, but instead is a strength.

Performing a kind act is an extraordinary way to feed my soul.

I release my fear and shyness and open my heart to others, offering a sincere smile and greeting to strangers without expecting anything in return.

One of my purposes for being alive today is to extend kindness to someone else.

I take a moment in silence to remind myself to act with kindness throughout the rest of the day.

My kindness springs from my soul, and my natural state of loving-kindness expands with my personal development.

I face my challenges with kindness rather than feeding the negative energy of a situation.

At any moment, I can close my eyes, breathe deeply, and call upon my inner reservoir of patience, humility, and kindness.

My natural reaction in every situation is kindness.

I am kind to myself by filling my mind with positive, inspiring thoughts.

I spread the energy of kindness by repeating touching stories of kindness that I have heard or witnessed. People are always ready to hear good news.

When I do a random act of kindness, I receive an abundance of positive energy from the universe.

Because I am a unique individual, I have my own style of spreading love and kindness. The world is a more interesting place because I extend kindness in my own way.

My positive thoughts fill my life with positive action.

I let go of the mean, selfish attitudes that close me off from my kind, natural self. From this moment on, I am an open vessel through which kindness can flow.

I am enormously positive in everything I think, do, and say.

The universe puts me in the paths of those who need to receive acts of kindness.

Kindness flows naturally from me.

I contain within me a never-ending source of kindness, gentleness, and compassion.

I feel wonderful when I treat someone with kindness.

Every act of kindness returns to me with even more positive energy.

I respect everyone's birthright to be treated with kindness and understanding.

I am completely at ease with my loving attitude, which allows me to freely offer kindness to others.

I respect and love myself unconditionally, and others love and respect me.

Everyone is precious and deserves to be treated with kindness.

I freely give compliments with sincerity and warmth. I release the thought that I can only add to my worth by breaking down the worth of another.

I always treat waiters, waitresses, airline attendants, clerks, and other service providers with cheerfulness, kindness, and respect.

Being kind is a choice.

My mind is constantly creating positive thoughts that spill over into my life as random acts of kindness.

I have a limitless capacity for kindness.

My relaxed, serene, and loving attitude motivates others to be kind and patient.

I radiate kindness in every situation.

My birthright as a human being is to approach life with compassion and kindness.

I am most effective when I speak gently and sincerely, and free myself from ego-centered reactions.

My soul is filled with kindness that longs to be expressed.

When I resist kindness and act out of anger and impatience, I quickly become aware of my actions and transform my negative behavior into sincere, selfless kindness.

All of my old habits and attitudes are simply memories, and I can replace them at any time with new habits of positive thoughts and kindness.

I am big enough to admit my mistakes without becoming defensive.

I find beautiful and moving examples of kindness everywhere I look.

All people are intrinsically kind and generous, and I do everything I can to continually bring out this quality in myself.

When I approach a stressful situation with kindness, I feel my heart open and know that I am drawing positive energy from the universe.

I never miss an opportunity to reverse the energy of a situation from negative to positive through kindness.

My inner self knows what to do at all times, and I trust that I will do the kind, compassionate thing if I listen to the quiet voice within.

My greatest strength lies in my reservoir of inner wisdom. I can tap into this resource at any time and any place.

I am grateful to be open to the loving energy of the universe.

I trust the invisible, silent place within me as much as I trust the unseen power of love.

My heart grows more open and loving every day.

One kind act can rejuvenate someone with hope, providing a gentle reminder that all is well in the universe.

No act of kindness is too small.

My commitment to being a kind, loving person draws extremely positive energy into my life.

No day is ever the same when I allow myself to express kindness to strangers, as well as to those I know and love.

When I act out of sincere kindness and compassion, I enter the flow of love that permeates all life.

I tap into my reservoir of love to bring it into the world through acts of kindness.

Every act of kindness is an expression of love, and everyone deserves to be loved.

I bring love into my home by anticipating work that needs to be done, and by cheerfully doing it without being asked.

I choose to be cheerful, and try to lift the spirit of every situation I am in. Bringing this bright energy into the world is an act of kindness.

There is no limit to the reservoir of love that resides within me, and I will never exhaust my power to be kind, patient, and compassionate.

I connect with others on the level of the soul when I approach them with genuine kindness.

I honor and extend kindness to myself by calmly dealing with my challenges and letting go of petty worries.

I always follow my natural instinct to do the kind, thoughtful thing.

Kindness is a habit that I nurture every day out of love for others.

8.

Compassion

When people do things that irritate me, I put myself in their shoes and try to understand them.

When I develop a bigger perspective, I gain compassion for people.

I have an unfailing center of compassion within me.

I remain in the moment when working with others, offering a competent and compassionate perspective at all times.

I take the time to understand the unique challenges facing my family members, friends, and coworkers.

I receive people with compassion, and see the innocence that lies within their souls.

I look beyond someone's behavior to find the joy, light, and innocence within.

I practice compassion by listening intently to others and giving them my complete attention.

Every moment spent expressing compassion for another is a holy moment.

My compassion allows me to transcend immediate annoyances and see beyond others' words and actions.

My deep and sincere compassion for others is an extension of my all-loving soul. When I express compassion, I reveal my natural state of loving-kindness.

I see the innocence in those with whom I do not agree and always keep an open mind.

Being compassionate connects me to my higher self.

When I take my attention away from the insignificant annoyances of the day, I open my heart to others and become more compassionate.

I am committed to acting in a compassionate way every day, even if it merely means offering a genuine smile to a stranger.

With practice, my compassion deepens, and my life becomes more rich.

Being compassionate helps me grow into a more peaceful, relaxed person.

My partner and I develop compassion for each other by taking the time to sit together in silence.

I take my attention off my small problems and consider the situations of others.

I recognize that other people's pain is as real as my own.

Opening my heart with compassion greatly enhances my sense of gratitude.

I am in awe of the life experiences of compassionate people, and derive inspiration from the challenges that they have overcome to gain such mastery.

Every day, I develop compassion through intention and action. I focus my mind on the needs of others, and put my actions where my heart is.

My compassion is always growing, deepening, and finding new outlets for expression.

Reflecting on the needs of others helps me get rid of my own excess baggage.

Before I begin my day, I ask my higher self to fill my heart with compassion so that I can be of service to others in any way, no matter how small, throughout the day.

By understanding others, I more fully understand myself.

I react to stressful situations with compassion, opening my mind to see all sides of the story and to understand every point of view.

My compassion is a sincere expression of the love in my heart.

I follow the examples of great masters of compassion and live every day trying to act with the same loving-kindness.

I choose to deal with others from my soul's deep well of compassion.

I am free at all times to ask my higher self for help in finding compassion when it appears that I am reacting out of selfishness or pettiness.

I maintain a calm, peaceful center at all times, and compassion naturally flows from this source.

Everything I do is an expression of the love of the Creator. I treat others as I would like to be treated, and my compassion flows freely and effortlessly.

The compassionate way I treat others is a barometer of my spiritual maturity and integrity.

Compassion is a practice that deepens and grows more powerful with time. I dedicate a few moments every day to connecting with my soul and strengthening my qualities of kindness, patience, humility, and compassion.

I am always open to acting with compassion because, as Mother Teresa said, "We cannot do great things on this earth. We can only do small things with great love."

My life is the creation of my mind. When I focus on compassion, I naturally relate to others with love and understanding.

I do not live in isolation; therefore, I have a choice in how I relate to others. I vow to exercise compassion in every situation.

When I act sincerely and from my soul, I automatically respond with compassion.

Compassion, like love, is its own reward.

Through compassion, I reach the highest peak of self-fulfillment.

Compassion is the vehicle for human and divine love to work in people's lives.

I am capable of enormous compassion, and I commit myself to developing this quality to its highest degree.

I bring higher energy into the world through my acts of compassion.

My soul fills me with a natural empathy for others, which helps me relate to everyone in a loving way.

By cultivating compassion, I reach deeper into my inner resources and connect more closely with my soul.

I practice compassion by wishing everyone well and releasing all feelings of envy, jealousy, and resentment.

Compassion is a gift that allows me to more freely spread the loving energy of the universe into the lives of those around me.

I practice compassion toward myself by giving myself time to feed my soul and clear my mind of negativity.

I truly desire to be a more compassionate person.

I possess everything that I need to awaken my unlimited compassion.

Compassion is an intrinsic part of my nature. My old habit of criticizing myself and others is now transformed into love and forgiveness.

My quiet mind is crystal-clear, allowing me to connect with my soul and act with compassion.

I always try to understand others and put myself in their shoes, rather than blindly judging and criticizing that which I do not understand.

Today is a once-in-a-lifetime opportunity to treat others with compassion.

I am much greater than my thinking, conscious mind, and I deal with people through the compassion of my heart.

I am grateful for the compassionate acts with which others have touched, healed, or improved my life.

Looking through the eyes of compassion allows me to see deeper into those that I love.

I look upon my past with compassion, and acknowledge that every experience has led me to this moment, bringing me clearer insight and awareness. I let go of all regrets.

I am constantly aware of the compassion that others feel toward me, and I am grateful for the love that connects us all.

Compassion brings me deeper into life, giving me a wider range of feelings.

I strive to be aware of my feelings so that I can be a more compassionate person.

My open, loving heart knows no bounds.

If I cannot help someone by physical or financial means, I hold that person in my heart with love.

I belong to the family of humankind, and I extend my love to everyone.

My compassion comes from a sincere desire to be loving.

The small acts of caring that I see around me inspire me to be more compassionate.

One of my highest goals is to develop compassion and express genuine caring for others.

My heart is filled with respect, patience, gentleness, generosity, and compassion.

9.

True Progress

When I think of one kind act that I did today, however small, I know I am moving forward in life.

The power to change anything in my life lies in my own mind. I choose to let go of self-defeating attitudes and replace them with positive thoughts.

Every moment, I am becoming more loving, more considerate of others, more generous, and more filled with positive thoughts.

I commit myself to the practice of quieting my mind and reflecting in silence, bringing myself closer to my soul and my highest potential.

There is nothing I cannot do if I put my mind to it.

The future awaits my dreams and the blueprint for success that I now create with my positive thoughts.

I keep score of my success by measuring how much I love, not by how many things I acquire.

I try my best to be kind and gentle in every situation, and I am becoming more loving every moment.

I no longer filter everything through anger, but let old resentments go and move into a brighter state of mind.

I improve the quality of my life with every positive thought.

What I begin to practice now will become second nature. The dreams I envision are unfolding every moment.

When I am very busy, I remember to take things one step at a time, and enjoy the feeling of each small accomplishment.

Every forward step I have made in my life gives me complete confidence in myself. I take the time to appreciate how far I've come.

Every day, I improve the emotional climate of my home and workplace.

I know that I am moving forward because I don't sweat the small stuff, and I am able to handle the big stuff with grace and dignity.

I celebrate each tiny step of progress, inspired by my self-discipline and integrity.

I expand my perspective and my capacity for understanding every day, always taking the time to see good things in everyone.

People recognize my deeper sense of calm, and are more comfortable around me every day.

Sincere warmth glows in my heart and brings me closer to those that I love.

Every morning, I vow to approach everything with an open heart and be even more loving than the day before.

I handle problems more easily than I did a month, a year, and a decade ago, because I am committed to becoming the best person I can be.

I choose to envision only peace, harmony, and kindness in my family.

I keep my mind focused on the positive, and I am excited about the future.

Nurturing my soul brings me rewards that overflow from my life into the lives of others.

Every day, I am better able to put myself in another person's place and understand another point of view.

My potential is only limited by my negative thoughts. Every day, positive thoughts take the place of negative ones and completely change my life.

My positive thoughts are capable of manifesting all of my dreams in the real world.

I transfer my energy from my external life to my inner knowing, and reap the rewards of living a soulful life.

I take time to acknowledge the still, quiet place within me and draw strength, compassion, and wisdom from it.

Every day, I achieve more balance between my mind and my soul. Everything in my life benefits from this harmony.

My life reflects the positive thoughts that come from my heart.

At the end of the day, I take time to reflect on how my actions made a difference to someone else, how I served others, and how much I loved. This is the measure of my true progress from moment to moment.

I am grateful for every step on my life path that has led me to the deeper wisdom and understanding I enjoy today.

I am excited about the next step in my self-development, and trust that I am moving forward at every moment.

The positive thoughts I produce now are creating a positive future for me and for those that I love.

Nothing about my past can block my future, because my new positive thoughts are all-powerful.

I have abundant enthusiasm for life, and look forward to each new day.

I have more than enough energy to work toward my dreams and help others in the process.

Being a source of love is one of the top priorities in my life.

Material success is just one automatic byproduct of my positive thoughts and open heart.

I release all feelings of failure, knowing that the glorious future is in my hands.

The loving, enthusiastic, and inspiring people in my life reflect the positive priorities I have set for myself.

As I grow more connected to my soul, I see more of the world's beauty.

As I open my heart and accept that change is part of life, I make room for new hobbies, interests, and career paths.

My higher self sees into my future and gives me hints that I am on the right path.

I spend my mind's energy wisely, trying to produce positive thoughts.

My mind holds the lock and key to my mental health and well-being.

I am dedicated to exploring my inner world and undertaking the greatest adventure in life—getting to know who I really am.

Yesterday is just a vanishing thought. Today I have the opportunity to start fresh and create miracles.

I realize that I am here for a brief moment, and I try to make the best of each day.

My path leads me to greater and greater happiness, and something marvelous is always right around the corner.

Every day, I find a way to contribute something, no matter how small, to the goodness of the world.

I am guided by my higher self, and everything I do has positive influence on the future.

My positive energy helps me turn away from the past and face the future with hope and anticipation.

Every day, I am more and more at ease.

The stress I have accumulated in my life is fading away with each breath.

I no longer force things to go my way, but instead, gently allow my inner knowledge to direct me. My old habit of controlling every second of my life is a thing of the past.

Everyone who comes into contact with me is refreshed by my positive energy.

My small steps of progress—coping with grace, not sweating the small stuff, putting everything into perspective, relating to others with kindness—are actually miraculous transformations.

I am not the person I was yesterday, but a more enlightened being.

My mind is filled with the certainty that everything is going according to life's plan, and that my inner wisdom is directing all of my steps.

My choices are always based on love, thoughtfulness, generosity, and compassion.

I listen to my inner voice, and always choose the right moment to make a change in thinking and doing.

One of the greatest measures of my progress is my ability to forgive myself.

During stressful times, I let go of the habit of complaining. My new thinking allows me to laugh at myself when I stumble; to brush myself off; and to move forward with renewed energy.

I am capable of more than I can possibly dream. I allow myself to think big, dream big, and live with a heart overflowing with love.

I strive to provide a positive example to help others focus on the most positive aspects of themselves.

Just like the technology in science fiction novels that has now become reality, I create positive thoughts that will come to fruition in their time.

My progress as a more loving person is a gift I give to the world.

I acknowledge my higher self as the captain of my life, and trust that great plans are at work.

Every time I handle stress with less anxiety, I am reminded of my great personal progress.

There are no obstacles I cannot overcome with my inner resources, and I take the time to pause and reflect on the outstanding results I have achieved with my positive thoughts and inner wisdom.

I fill every aspect of my life—work, romance, family, recreation, study—with enormous positive energy.

I mark my progress by how calm and peaceful I remain when someone keeps me waiting, when I lose something, when someone abuses me for no reason, or when I make a clumsy mistake. When one of these things occurs in my life, I recall how I reacted to the same situation a year ago and congratulate myself on my progress.

I am grateful for the lessons that have helped me dig into my inner resources to find my real strength and peace of mind.

I am perfectly aligned with my inner wisdom, and always know what to do.

I value my soul connection and invest time in being alone, quiet, and peaceful. One measure of my personal progress is how well I nurture my soul.

I act upon my positive thoughts and let go of procrastination.

I am responsible for my progress, and I am filled with self-discipline and enthusiasm.

I always have an open mind, and people look to me for creative solutions to problems.

I appreciate the riches of life that are available to me right now.

Every day, I am more filled with positive energy, and people are drawn to my special light.

I receive all the support and inspiration that I need from my inner wisdom, and this voice constantly gives me encouragement along my journey.

Every positive thought is an investment in my better future.

I feel my burden getting lighter with each positive thought.

I let go of my fears and worries about money, and enter into a new relationship with abundance. From this day forward, my financial life is prosperous and ever-growing.

The love and kindness I express returns to me, and my future is filled with echoes of my positive thoughts.

My progress is marked by my ability to put my ego and my own thoughts aside when listening to others. Mindful listening is a powerful form of compassion.

I have such profound trust in my inner wisdom that I start each day expecting a miracle. The most amazing miracles in my life are my ability to love and to receive love.

I take the time to do the things that I love because my soul work is as important as all the other work I do.

I contain all of the vitality and energy to live each day to its fullest.

My peaceful surrender to worry or fear allows me to sleep deeply through the night and wake refreshed every morning. I am free of anxiety at all times.

I am always in contact with my inner wisdom, and I remain calm and peaceful in stressful situations. I provide a positive example to others during a dispute at home or at work.

Nothing negative in my past has the power to affect my life today. This moment is created out of my positive thoughts, and only good things can come to me.

I am filled with positive energy that makes me a wonderful friend, partner, and coworker.

My vital positive energy draws all good things to me.

I close each day with gratitude for the progress I have made in becoming a more loving human being.

I am grateful to everyone who has brought positive energy into my life and helped me move more swiftly on my path.

Even the smallest act of kindness is a major step on my journey toward perfect peace.

There is no limit to the power of my positive thoughts, and I am open to all good things. My future is filled with adventure, wonder, love, harmony, and countless blessings.

10.

In the Moment

I am always focused on the moment, which allows me to work, play, and live with relaxed passion rather than hyperactive frenzy.

My ideas and creativity thrive when I am clearly focused in the present.

There is only this moment, right now. The quality that I bring to it defines the quality of my life.

No problem is more important than my happiness and inner peace.

My life should not be approached as a to-do list, but as a gift.

I do not view problems as great obstacles to avoid, but as inevitable parts of life.

I approach everything I do with centered, focused attention on the present, and enjoy great joy and success.

I am oriented in the present moment when I am with others, and I'm genuinely interested in them.

I surrender to the reality that life is exactly as it should be in this moment.

Life is a series of new feelings in every new moment, and this moment, I have the opportunity to transform my life with a positive new outlook.

I do not get stuck in past behaviors or experiences, because those moments are over forever.

I express my intentions with intensity at this moment, and trust that the universe is molding my positive thoughts into reality.

I close my eyes and feel the joy of being alive in this moment.

I am calmly centered in the moment, and this spreads peace to those around me.

When I put my full, loving concentration on what I am doing, I live completely in the moment, and time seems to stop.

I remain centered in the moment, and everything gets done at a leisurely, sane pace.

My mind is always focused on the present, and I do every task one at a time, calmly, as it arises.

The high energy I receive by being fully in the present motivates me to return to this center throughout the day.

My practice of staying in the present opens up a new, ever-expanding world of possibilities.

I close my eyes, focus on the here and now, and savor this moment.

My emotions pass through my life from moment to moment, and I always have the choice to transform anger, resentment, envy, and criticism into positive emotions of forgiveness, acceptance, and compassion.

Each moment is a new beginning.

It is never too late to change my thinking and change my life. Everything is possible in this moment.

I bring equanimity into my life with a focus on the present, and this relieves stress in me and in those around me.

I accept what is actually occurring in the moment—this is a profound form of wisdom.

I am engaged in the here and now, rather than keeping score from the sidelines.

I live my life, not as a rehearsal, but as happening fully in this moment, right now.

I focus my mind on the sensations and details of this moment, clearing my mind of all distractions, and giving my full energy to the task at hand.

During holidays, birthdays, and other traditional celebrations, I stay focused on the present moment rather than comparing the day to events in the past. I appreciate and experience the moment for what it is, not for what it may be or should be.

I do not entertain the thought, "I will be happy when..." but accept my happiness and fullness of life in this moment.

I practice the gift of presence by being lovingly, patiently in the moment, whether I am with a stranger, a family member, or a friend.

One of the most magical gifts I can give another is being fully present, listening with my entire being.

I care about people as individuals, and I am always present when I communicate.

I release myself from my repeated, circular thinking—my "hamster wheel"—and live only in this moment.

I try to deal with everything that arises with an open mind, because I am centered in the here and now.

The magic of change and transformation pours into my life when I focus on the present and leave all distractions behind.

Every moment is an invitation to quiet my mind and experience who I really am.

I pause every day to experience the immediate and intimate reality of the present moment.

This moment is the perfect essence of my life. I choose to experience the reality of now, just as it is.

The quality of my attention in this moment is more important than my goals, my destinations, or my journey.

I live completely in the moment and release my habit of restless searching for answers outside of myself.

My actions are based upon clear, spontaneous impulses, not upon fear from past experiences.

I allow things to happen in the moment rather than forcing them to happen with worry and other desperate thoughts.

This is the perfect time to slow down and be aware of what is happening right now.

Life is a series of moments, and I am fully present in each one.

My here-and-now focus creates enormous vitality and clarity.

My focus on the present allows me to hear the still, quiet voice that holds all of my answers.

I take control and focus on the moment, releasing my old habit of musing about the past and worrying about the future.

I live each moment of my life with value and purpose.

The cobwebs of regret and frustration and thoughts of "could have" are cleared away in this moment.

The glorious vitality of now fills my mind.

When I feel overwhelmed, I pause to remember that this is a fleeting moment, and I have the power to choose to experience it calmly and peacefully.

I am invited to have a second chance, a third chance—limitless chances—at becoming the best I can be by living each moment in the present.

My senses are heightened when I focus on the here and now.

I am a powerfully positive, wonderful force in the universe at this moment.

Nothing can hold me back from releasing positive, enthusiastic thoughts right now.

The thread of my life is made of countless moments strung side by side. I choose to experience those moments in full consciousness, living life to its fullest, rather than working toward perfecting one or two moments at the expense of all the others.

I always bring my full attention to my work, my play, and those that I love.

Everything is possible in this perfect, flawless moment.

I am open and receptive to the creative ideas of the universe.

My mind is no longer a dumping ground for regrets and worries, but is instead a clear, fresh open space where positive thoughts flow.

The rest of my life depends on the quality of this moment, because the rest of my life is only a series of moments.

I am grateful for the self-discipline that allows me to pause and savor this moment. With each success of attaining this peaceful state, I improve my ability to remain in the present.

My ability to stay in the moment fills me with a constant stream of positive energy.

Focusing on what I am doing helps me slip into the timelessness of pure creativity.

My mind is clean and pure, open to all good things.

Focusing on the present helps me explore the mysterious reality beneath my everyday thoughts and distractions.

One of the greatest gifts of the universe is my clear, present awareness.

I am capable of living in the perfect calm that I see in nature.

My mind is ready and willing to let go of all thoughts.

This moment, I clear my mind of anger, sadness, anxiety, envy, frustration, cynicism, worry, and regret.

I choose to devote a few moments each day to stopping everything and focusing on the moment. This practice will overflow into the rest of my life with very positive results.

My attention is on the present, and I am keenly aware of every sound, scent, and color around me.

There is no limit to the adventure and discovery that awaits me within.

I fully accept that this moment is the only reality that exists.

I refuse to submit to the habit of playing old tapes in my mind.

I choose to clear my thoughts, relax, take a breath, and simply be.

I am lovable and worthy of all good things just as I am.

I make conscious decisions because I am focused on the here and now.

I absorb the serenity and power of this moment in all of its glory.

I deal with change on a moment-to-moment basis, and I am always ready to follow the perfect path for each situation.

My calm state of mind is a pool of limitless ideas and creativity.

Practicing being in the moment allows me to derive deeper pleasure and appreciation for everything that I do and everything that crosses my path.

I open myself to the vast, unknown territory of the present moment.

I no longer blow the small stuff out of proportion, because my mind is focused on the present. In this state of mind, everything is seen in its proper perspective.

Life is rarely exactly what I would like it to be, but it is always precisely what it is. I accept this with openness and grace.

My mind is eager to follow a new adventure and focus on the miracle of the present.

The quality of my life improves from the inside out as I practice living in the present.

Every day, I see more clearly that it is pointless and irrational to dwell on the past or worry about the future.

Committing myself to practices such as focusing on the present and letting go of worry increases my self-respect and self-confidence.

My overactive mind deserves to be given a break.

Clearing my mind is as purposeful as using it to do my job or take care of my responsibilities.

My practice of living in the moment helps me view others as clear, innocent beings who are also living from one moment to another.

Clearing my mind of negative thoughts relieves stress and makes me better able to handle any conflict, large or small.

I understand that everyone, including me, is capable of dramatic transformation. Each moment provides a new chance to make a fresh start.

I practice mindful communication, which is closer to living in the moment than listening and thinking to myself at the same time. This form of listening is deeply respectful and honors others.

Each morning, I renew my commitment to focus on the present. With practice, my mind is becoming clearer, and it is easier to reach this state of just being.

Every day, I am grateful to be alive and pause to appreciate and simply behold the moment.

There is nothing more precious than the love I feel in my heart right now.

With my ever-deepening practice and development, it becomes harder and harder to sweat the small stuff.

My Own Affirmations

My Own Affirmations